CASS BECOMES A STAR

MW00568582

Many advertisements
and television commercials
have animals in them.
Have you ever wondered
how those animals came to be there?

This is Cass,
a yellow Labrador retriever,
who is three years old.
She starred in a television commercial.
And this is the story
of how she did it.

Cass lives in the country.
Her owner, Dave,
has spent a lot of time training her.
He is kind and gentle,
and Cass has learned to obey
a lot of commands.
She will come when called,
and, when told, she will sit still,
stay in one place, or lie down.
And she loves to do
what all retrievers do best:
retrieve or fetch things.

One day, Dave saw an advertisement
in a newspaper
for an animal acting agency.
He wrote to them,
and they sent him a form to fill in.
He wrote down everything
that Cass could do
and sent the form back.
Not long after, Dave got a phone call.
Cass was wanted for a part
in a television commercial.

On the day of the shoot,
Cass got into her special trailer
and was driven to the location.
It was an empty football stadium.
Cass had to wear a football jersey
and pretend to be in a crowd
watching a football game.
She met one of the principal actors
and then joined about twenty other people
who were pretending to be part
of a crowd.
They had to imagine
that a football game was being played,
and to shout and cheer when told.

After everyone was told what to do,
the scene was shot.
The cameraman filmed Cass and the people,
while the sounds they made were recorded.

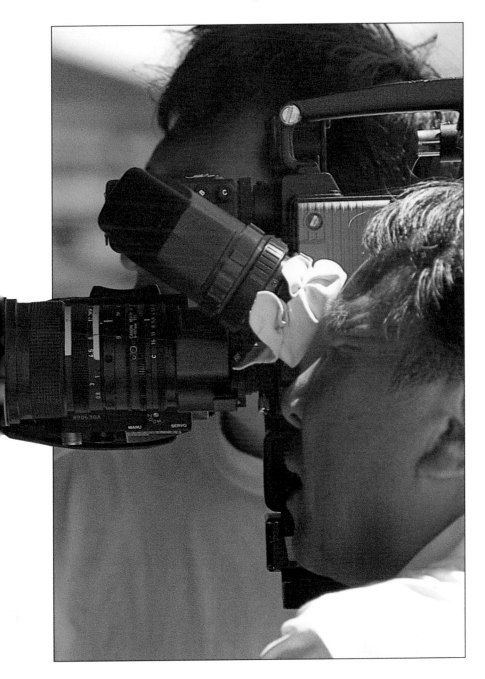

After that, Cass had to lean forward
and eat some food
from the actors' yellow bag.
She enjoyed that
because they had to film it several times,
and each time she got something to eat.
For the last shot,
she had to pull the bag away.
It was difficult, but she finally managed it.

When it was all over,
the film that had been recorded
was played back on a video recorder
so that the director could see it
and make sure it was all right.
Cass watched too.

For the next scene,
she had to carry the yellow bag
out through the stadium entrance.
She did it right the first time.
All the people watching clapped.

15

After that, everyone got into buses and cars and drove to a new location. It was a park. Cass watched and waited while the camera crew set up their equipment.

She also made some more friends.
Then it was time for her
to act out another scene.

She had to sit still,
then run to Dave when he called her.
He was out of sight,
so in the film it would look as if
she was just running through the park.
She had to do that twice,
because the first time she didn't run straight.
But the second time, she did it perfectly.

In the last scene,
Cass had to run to Dave again.
But this time,
it was in a different part of the park,
and she had to carry the yellow bag.
She did it right the first time.
Everyone cheered for her
and clapped their hands.
She was a star!

Then it was all over and time to leave.
When she got home, Dave gave her a big hug
and an extra-special dinner.
She ate it all in about one minute.

Cass had enjoyed her day, but she was tired.
Soon she had fallen fast asleep.
Perhaps she dreamed about all the things
that had happened that day,
and the people she had met.
But one thing was certain: she was now a star!

And as for Dave,
he couldn't wait to see Cass on TV.